Steve Jobs

Children's Literacy Foundation

cl_if

This is my book!

clif@clifonline.org ★ www.clifonline.org ★ 802.244.0944

JOSH GREGORY

Children's Press®
An Imprint of Scholastic Inc.
New York Toronto London Auckland Sydney
Mexico City New Delhi Hong Kong
Danbury, Connecticut

Content Consultant
James Marten, PhD
Professor and Chair, History Department
Marquette University
Milwaukee, Wisconsin

Library of Congress Cataloging-in-Publication data

Gregory, Josh.
  Steve Jobs/Josh Gregory.
      p. cm.—(A true book)
  Includes bibliographical references and index.
  ISBN 978-0-531-21907-2 (lib. bdg.) — ISBN 978-0-531-23878-3 (pbk.)
1. Jobs, Steve, 1955–2011—Juvenile literature. 2. Computer engineers—United States—
Biography—Juvenile literature. 3. Businesspeople—United States—Biography—Juvenile litera-
ture. 4. Apple Computer, Inc.—History—Juvenile literature. I. Title.
  QA76.2.J63G74 2013
  621.39092—dc23 [B]   2012036049

All rights reserved. Published in 2013 by Children's Press, an imprint of Scholastic Inc.
Printed in the United States of America 113
SCHOLASTIC, CHILDREN'S PRESS, A TRUE BOOK™, and associated logos are trademarks and/or
registered trademarks of Scholastic Inc.
1 2 3 4 5 6 7 8 9 10 R 22 21 20 19 18 17 16 15 14 13

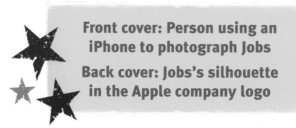
**Front cover: Person using an
iPhone to photograph Jobs**

**Back cover: Jobs's silhouette
in the Apple company logo**

Find the Truth!

Everything you are about to read is true *except* for one of the sentences

Which one is **TRUE**?

T or F Steve Jobs designed and built the Apple II computer on his own.

T or F Steve Jobs once worked for the video game company Atari.

Find the answers in this book.

Contents

THE **BIG** TRUTH!

Daring Designs

Steve Jobs and Steve Wozniak display the Apple I computer.

4 A Second Chance

Apple receives 30 percent of all money earned from iTunes sales.

Steve Jobs helped create many of today's most popular electronic devices.

Early Days

On February 24, 1955, a young mother named Joanne Schieble welcomed her first child into the world. Schieble and the baby's father had decided not to keep the newborn boy. A couple named Paul and Clara Jobs, who had been unable to have children of their own, adopted the child. Paul and Clara named their new son Steven Paul Jobs. Little did they know that he would one day change the world.

Steve Jobs was well known for unveiling new products with thrilling presentations.

Silicon Valley

Steve Jobs spent most of his youth in an area of California known as Silicon Valley. Silicon is a material used to create electronic devices. Silicon Valley gets its name from the many electronic technology companies located there. Living there gave Steve a close look at how new technology was created. Many of his neighbors were engineers at local tech companies. They sometimes showed their projects to young Steve.

Silicon Valley is home to many major technology companies, including Apple.

Jobs's love of carefully designed products began with watching his father work on projects at their home.

Learning Lessons

Steve learned about building things by watching his father. Paul Jobs enjoyed fixing up old cars in his garage. He showed his son the importance of making even the smallest details of a project perfect.

In high school, Steve joined a group of students interested in electronics. Engineers from the nearby Hewlett-Packard Company often presented their latest projects to the group. At one presentation, Steve saw a desktop computer for the first time.

Hewlett and Packard started their company in a one-car garage.

Bill Hewlett (left) founded Hewlett-Packard with David Packard (right).

Steve was a hard worker. In high school, he had a newspaper route and worked as a salesman at an electronics store. One summer, he worked in the Hewlett-Packard factory. Bill Hewlett, the **CEO** of Hewlett-Packard, had given him the job. Steve had looked Hewlett up in the phone book and called him because he needed parts for an electronic device he was building. Hewlett was so impressed that he immediately offered Steve a job.

A New Friend

During his junior year of high school, Steve took an electronics class. One of his classmates introduced him to a friend who had graduated from their high school a couple of years earlier. His name was Steve Wozniak, but most people knew him simply as "Woz." Woz and Steve Jobs liked each other immediately. They both loved electronics, and they spent hours chatting about new technology and listening to their favorite music.

Woz (left) and Steve (right) bonded over their shared love of computers and rock music.

Woz

Like Steve, Woz had been interested in electronics since he was very young. However, he had a much stronger knowledge of electronics than Steve did. One of Woz's most impressive early projects was an intercom system. The system was used throughout the neighborhood by his friends. Woz designed his first computer when he was still in high school. He was working for a computer company when he met Steve.

Woz was even better at building electronic devices than Steve was.

Steve and Woz's first profitable invention was a phone dialing device.

Steve and Woz worked on electronic devices together in their spare time. One of their creations was a box that allowed them to make telephone calls. Steve thought they could make money by building more boxes and selling them. He estimated that each box would cost $40 to build. The two scraped together some money and built 100 boxes. They sold all of them for $150 each, their first business success.

Jobs briefly attended Reed College in Portland, Oregon.

Off to College

When Jobs graduated from high school in 1972, he wasn't sure if he wanted to go to college. Under pressure from his parents, however, Jobs decided to attend Reed College in Portland, Oregon. He officially dropped out just a few months after starting, but he continued to attend his favorite classes even though he was not a student. Eventually, in February 1974, he moved back to his parents' house in Silicon Valley.

Working at Atari

Jobs soon found work at the video game company Atari. His bosses liked him, but he did not get along well with most of his co-workers. Because he did not shower often, he usually smelled bad. He also tended to insult people when he didn't think they were doing good work. Jobs's bosses at Atari eventually asked him to work at night so other employees wouldn't have to spend time with him.

Jobs wrote this note while working on a project at Atari.

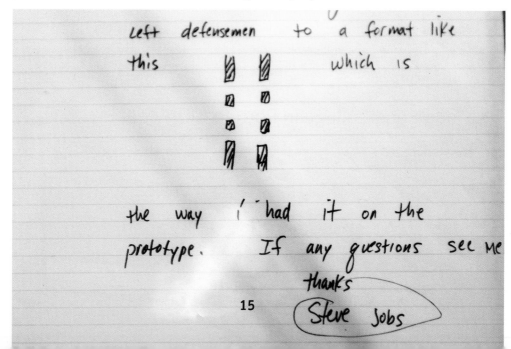

15

A Revolutionary Idea

In 1975, Wozniak saw the new Altair 8800, a cutting-edge computer available for computer hobbyists and businesses. It was operated by switches, which caused lights on the front panel to light up. Wozniak was amazed by the power of the Altair's small **microprocessor**. He decided he could use such a microprocessor to build a computer small enough to fit on a desk. Even inexperienced users could connect a keyboard and monitor to the device.

Wozniak saw potential in the Altair 8800's capabilities.

The two Steves worked together closely to build the first Apple computer.

Wozniak completed a **prototype** of his computer on June 29, 1975. As he typed on the keyboard, letters appeared on his monitor. Wozniak's device impressed everyone who saw it, including Jobs. Jobs suggested ways to improve the prototype. More importantly, he encouraged Wozniak to keep the computer's design a secret. He believed the new computer could make the two friends a lot of money. Wozniak and Jobs started a company to make and sell the computers. They called it Apple Computer.

Apple I users had to build their
own cases, such as this wooden
one, from scratch.

CHAPTER 2

Making It Big

Jobs and Wozniak called their first computer **model** the Apple I. Their first sale was to a local electronics shop, which purchased 50 Apple I computers. These early models did not look anything like the sleek machines for which Apple later became known. Instead, the models were sold as simple **circuit boards**. Users had to provide their own cases, keyboards, and monitors. Still, many people were impressed by how powerful the little machines were.

 In 2012, an original Apple I computer was sold at auction for $374,500.

A New Model

Wozniak soon began creating a new computer called the Apple II. It had many new features and was even able to display color images on a monitor. Jobs thought the new computer should come built into a visually appealing case. It would cost a lot of money to build such cases, though. Jobs solved this problem by convincing an investor to provide the company with $200,000.

Jobs put a great deal of thought into every detail of the Apple II's case.

The Apple II

Wozniak and Jobs first released the Apple II in April 1977. They sold 2,500 of the new computers by the end of that year. The Apple II was one of the company's biggest sellers until it stopped being made in the early 1990s. Several improved versions of the Apple II were released throughout its life span, adding new features and updated designs. By the time Apple discontinued the Apple II, more than 16 million had been sold.

The Apple II made Jobs and Wozniak famous among computer users everywhere.

Jobs named one of his computer designs "Lisa" after his first daughter.

Lisa

In 1977, soon after the release of the Apple II, Jobs reconnected with his high school girlfriend, Chrisann Brennan. Chrisann soon became pregnant. Jobs did not want a child, though. He was too wrapped up in his work at Apple to start a family. He broke up with Chrisann. Their daughter, Lisa, was born on May 17, 1978. Jobs did not have much contact with her for the first several years of her life.

The Macintosh

By the beginning of the 1980s, Apple had grown into a fairly large company with many employees. Wozniak worked mainly on improving the Apple II. Jobs led Apple's engineers in creating entirely new computers. One of these new computers was called the Macintosh. It contained a computer and a monitor all in one case. Jobs wanted it to be very easy to set up and use, even for beginners.

The Macintosh was designed to be small enough to fit on a desk in a home office.

The Macintosh had a unique **interface**. The image on the screen was designed to look like a desk. Files were represented with icons, or symbols, that users could click on and move around the screen with a mouse. This made it easy for even inexperienced users to perform a variety of tasks.

The Macintosh was a huge hit when it was released in January 1984. However, many users began reporting problems with the computers overheating, and sales decreased.

Large numbers of Macintosh computers were manufactured to meet the early demand.

Out of Work

Jobs grew more difficult
to work with. Many
of Apple's employees
complained that he made
it hard for them to do
their jobs. Apple's board
of directors, the group
of people chosen to make important decisions for
the company, knew they had to do something about
Jobs. They tried forcing him into a new position in
which he would have less control over the company.
He turned down the offer. In September 1985, he
resigned from, or left, Apple.

25

NeXT provided Jobs with a new
opportunity to change the way
people used computers.

CHAPTER 3

Two New Companies

Jobs was sad to leave the company he had helped build. But he knew he had no other choice if he wanted to continue leading the development of new projects. Almost immediately after leaving Apple, Jobs started a new company called NeXT. He staffed the company with former Apple employees he respected and with whom he got along. Together, they set about creating a new computer.

 NeXT computers were used in the creation of the World Wide Web.

The NeXT Step

Jobs wanted to design the NeXT computer for university students and professors. It would come with built-in books, including a dictionary and the complete works of William Shakespeare. It would also be powerful enough for use in advanced science experiments. Released in 1989, the NeXT computer was too expensive for most colleges to afford. As a result, it did not sell well. NeXT stopped making computers the following year but continued to work on the company's **operating system**.

The NeXT computer's black, cube-shaped case set it apart from other computers available at the time.

Jobs (on the right on the front sofa) poses with the other members of the Pixar team.

Pixar

NeXT was not Jobs's only new business after leaving Apple. In the fall of 1985, he purchased the computer graphics division of Lucasfilm, the company owned by *Star Wars* creator George Lucas. After purchasing the division, Jobs renamed it Pixar. At first, Pixar focused on building **hardware** and **software** that could be used to create advanced computer graphics.

The short films by John Lasseter (right) helped Jobs (center) realize Pixar's true strength. Fellow Pixar leader Edwin Catmull is on the left.

Some Pixar employees enjoyed using the company's technology to create short animated films. One of the workers, John Lasseter, had once been a Disney animator. Jobs was impressed by Lasseter's work and encouraged him to make more films. In 1986, Lasseter's *Luxo Jr.* was nominated for an Academy Award. Jobs realized that Pixar's true strength was not creating hardware and software. It was making films.

Going Hollywood

In 1995, Pixar released *Toy Story*, its first full-length animated film. The movie earned incredible reviews from almost all of the nation's top film critics. It was also a massive hit among audiences, making more money than any other film released that year. Since then, Pixar has released a long string of successful movies, from *A Bug's Life* (1998) to *Brave* (2012).

Toy Story and its sequels are among the most popular movies ever made.

Daring Designs

Steve Jobs's products have long been known for their unique designs. Here are some of the most famous ones.

Macintosh Computer (1984)

The original Macintosh computer was one of the first computers to include a built-in monitor. Jobs obsessed over every detail of the design, from the shape of the computer's corners to the color of its plastic.

NeXT Computer (1989)

Jobs designed the NeXT computer as a perfect cube. This made it difficult for the company's engineers to arrange the parts inside the case.

iMac (1998)

This was one of Jobs's first new products after returning to Apple. The first iMac had a rounded shape and a colorful, see-through case. It eventually became available in 11 solid colors and 2 patterns. It was also one of the first products Jobs created with the designer Jony Ive.

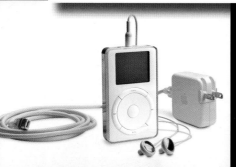

iPod (2001)

Another collaboration with Jony Ive, the iPod became a huge hit in part because of its simple, wheel-shaped controls.

Jobs and his wife Laurene
attend the 2010 Academy

A Second Chance

One evening in 1989, Jobs arrived at the Stanford Business School in California to speak to a group of students. There, he met Laurene Powell. They went on a date later that night. The couple wed on March 18, 1991. Around this time, Jobs's daughter Lisa came to live with them. The couple also had three children together. Their son Reed was born in 1991, their daughter Erin in 1995, and their daughter Eve in 1998.

Jobs asked Laurene Powell to marry him on New Year's Day 1990.

Selling NeXT

In 1996, Apple approached Jobs and offered to purchase NeXT. Apple wanted to use some of NeXT's operating system technology in its new computers. Jobs agreed to sell. He and most of NeXT's top employees once again began working at Apple.

Apple computers were not selling well at the time. The company fired its CEO in 1997 and offered the position to Jobs. He turned it down at first but accepted in September 1997.

Timeline of Jobs's Life

1955

Steve Jobs is born in San Francisco, California.

1977

Jobs and Steve Wozniak release the Apple II computer.

Turning Apple Around

Soon after returning to Apple, Jobs met Jony Ive, a designer who had been working at the company for several years. Ive shared many of Jobs's ideas about design. He quickly gained Jobs's respect. The pair went on to create many of the most famous Apple products of the 1990s and 2000s. One of their first projects was the iMac, based on Jobs's original Macintosh computer. Along with other products, the iMac helped put Apple back on the path to success.

1985
Jobs leaves Apple to found NeXT and Pixar.

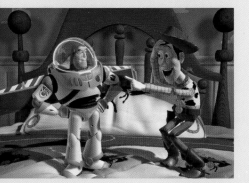

2011
Jobs dies after a long battle with cancer.

1997
Jobs returns to Apple.

Songs in Your Pocket

In 2000, Jobs began planning Apple's next big move. He wanted Apple to be part of the music industry. January 2001 saw the release of iTunes, Apple's program for playing music and copying CDs. Later that year, the company released the iPod. People could use these tiny music players to

carry all of their favorite songs wherever they went. In 2003, Apple added a store feature to iTunes, allowing users to purchase music online.

Jobs unveiled the iTunes store at a 2003 presentation.

Going Shopping

One of the biggest changes Steve Jobs made after taking over Apple was to design and build a series of **retail** stores. The first Apple store opened for business on May 19, 2001. Since then, hundreds of new Apple stores have been built in countries around the world. The stores allow people to try out the latest Apple devices for themselves. Customers can also bring in their Apple products for repairs and **upgrades**.

Customers try out the latest iPods at an Apple store in China.

Millions of people use iPhones today.

Making a Call

Jobs had another big idea in 2005. He asked Apple engineers to begin working on a new version of the iPod that could also be used as a cell phone. They based their design around a touch screen that allowed users to control the phone by making different finger movements. The device was named the iPhone. It could also be used to browse the Internet, play games, and run a variety of applications, or apps.

At Your Fingertips

Steve Jobs's final big project at Apple was a device called an iPad. It is a tablet computer that looks and functions very much like a larger version of the iPhone. The iPad has been one of his most successful creations for Apple. Today, people use iPads for everything from watching movies and playing games to downloading apps that help them run their businesses.

As of 2012, there were more than 170,000 available apps that were specifically made for the iPad.

41

An Unfortunate Ending

In 2003, Steve Jobs was diagnosed with cancer. He did not want surgery at first. After around nine months, the cancer had grown too much to ignore. He had an operation, but his doctors could not remove all of the cancer. He continued working at Apple even as he grew weaker over the next few years. By early 2011, he finally had to stop working. He died on October 5, 2011.

Fans around the world mourned Jobs's death.

You will be missed Steve
-Austin, USA

Steve Jobs changed the way people use computers.

A Remarkable Legacy

Apple fans around the world were saddened to hear about Jobs's death. Apple added a feature to its Web site that allowed people to post their thoughts about his influence. Thousands of people replied.

Though Jobs died at the relatively young age of 56, he accomplished an incredible amount over the course of his life. Without him, the music, cell phone, personal computer, and tablet computer industries would all be very different today. ★

True Statistics

Day Jobs was born: February 24, 1955

Number of Apple II computers sold in the first year: 2,500

Total number of Apple II computers sold: Around 16 million

Price of an Apple II computer in 1977: $1,298

Total ticket sales for all of Pixar's feature films (as of 2012): $3,031,274,537

Number of songs downloaded from the iTunes store since its launch (as of 2011): More than 10 billion

Number of iPods sold (as of 2011): More than 275 million

Did you find the truth?

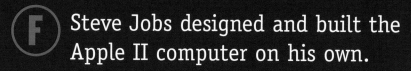
F Steve Jobs designed and built the Apple II computer on his own.

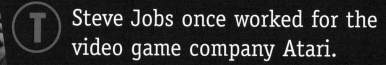
T Steve Jobs once worked for the video game company Atari.

Resources

Books

Lakin, Patricia. *Steve Jobs: Thinking Differently*. New York: Aladdin, 2012.

Pollack, Pam and Meg Belviso. *Who Was Steve Jobs?* New York: Grosset & Dunlap, 2012.

Venezia, Mike. *Steve Jobs & Steve Wozniak: Geek Heroes Who Put the Personal in Computers*. New York: Children's Press, 2010.

Ziller, Amanda. *Steve Jobs: American Genius*. New York: Collins, 2012.

Visit this Scholastic Web site for more information on Steve Jobs:
★ www.factsfornow.scholastic.com
Enter the keywords **Steve Jobs**

Important Words

CEO (SEE-EE-OH) — stands for chief executive officer, the person in charge of decision making in a company or organization

circuit boards (SUR-kit BORDZ) — pieces of plastic that have electrical circuits, or paths, printed onto them in the form of small metal strips

hardware (HAHRD-wair) — computer equipment, such as a printer, monitor, or keyboard

interface (IN-tur-fase) — a method of interacting with a computer system

microprocessor (mye-kroh-PRAH-ses-ur) — a computer chip that controls the functions of an electronic device

model (MAH-duhl) — a particular type or design of a product

operating system (AH-puh-ray-ting SIS-tuhm) — a master control program on a computer that allows other programs to run on the computer

prototype (PROH-tuh-type) — the first version of an invention that tests an idea to see if it will work

retail (REE-tayl) — related to the sale of goods to customers

software (SAWFT-wair) — computer programs

upgrades (UP-graydz) — the replacement of a computer part or piece of software with a better, more powerful, or more recently released version

Index

Page numbers in **bold** indicate illustrations.

About the Author

Josh Gregory writes and edits books for kids. He lives in Chicago, Illinois.